SUMS FOR SMART KIDS

BY LAURIE BUXTON

Published by BEAM Education, 2001
Maze Workshops
72a Southgate Road
London N1 3JT

tel: 020 7684 3323
fax: 020 7684 3334
email: info@beam.co.uk

www.beam.co.uk

Text copyright © 2001 Laurie Buxton
Illustrations by Paula Lewis
Edited by Jacky Rodger

Thanks to Mark Wainwright of Cambridge University and Dr Ian Redfern,
formerly of Cambridge and Warwick Universities, for their helpful comments
and enthusiastic support.

Printed by Latimer Trend & Company, Plymouth, Great Britain

British Library Cataloguing-in-Publication Data
A catalogue record for this book is available from the British Library
ISBN 1 903142 22 9

CONTENTS

INTRODUCTION

There is no single thing called 'intelligence'. We all have a range of mind skills, differently developed in each of us. This book is aimed at those with mathematical interests. Some mathematically gifted people are general all-rounders. Others are good only at mathematics. A person with a strong mathematical bent may be good at creative writing or may be unable to string words together. He or she may be physically adept or totally ham-handed, artistically gifted or unappreciative of any art form.

What the mathematically gifted do have in common is that they understand new concepts in the subject with remarkable rapidity. Mathematics is unusual in that there is little to remember but a great deal to understand.

This book offers the reader challenges to really engage with and extend their mathematical thinking even further. The problems are quite hard and will be found challenging by most young mathematicians, but they require no extra mathematical background. They are based on only very elementary mathematical facts.

ODD AND EVEN

For this chapter you only need to know the meaning of odd and even.

These are odd numbers: 1, 3, 5, 7, 9...

And these are even numbers: 2, 4, 6, 8, 10...

Before we start, let us establish some simple facts about odds and evens.

If we add two odd numbers the result is even. That is,

$O + O = E$

Please complete the following.

$O − O =$

$E + E =$

$E − E =$

$E + O =$

$E − O =$

$O − E =$

$O \times O =$

$E \times O =$

$E \times E =$

When you are sure of all of these, turn over.

(I am not going to tell anyone as clever as you the answers to the above; if you are not sure, give up now!)

THE MILK-CRATE PROBLEM

When you are older, you will know this as the beer-crate problem! The problem is not very hard, but there is an important point to be made.

Here is the crate, which has four rows and six columns.

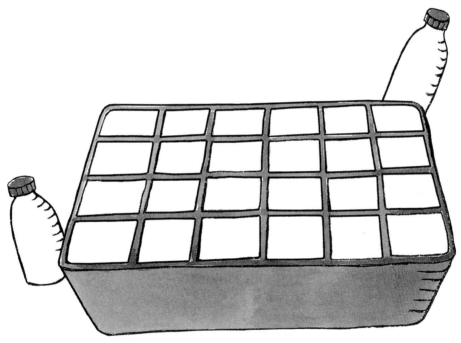

You have to place eighteen bottles in the crate in such a way that every row and every column has an even number of bottles. You may count zero as an even number.

So try it, and get someone else to check your answer.

When you are quite happy, start to think again and see if there is a much easier way of doing it. Do not turn over till you have found one. That is the real problem.

THE MILK-CRATE PROBLEM

Well, then, it was not too hard to find a solution. Here are two, but there are plenty more.

We can use trial and error, and this is perfectly all right in mathematics. Some problems about numbers rely on reducing the question to a few different possible answers, which we try in turn.

What, then, was the easy way?

Instead of placing the eighteen bottles, let's try thinking about the six gaps. These also have to come to an even number in every row and column, but working with the number 6 is very much easier than working with 18! Just try it and see.

In this problem we say that 6 is the COMPLEMENT of 18, and we shall find that some problems depend on working with a complement.

You can learn from this example to look for the same idea in other problems and make it part of your armoury.

THE BUNGALOW

In this one-storey house every room has an even number of doors. We only count doors that lead either to another room or out of the bungalow. Forget about cupboards.

Prove that there must be an even number of doors leading out.

VARIATION

A girl goes through every room of the bungalow and counts the doors in each room, keeping a running total. Show that if her final total is even, there are an even number of outer doors; and if it is odd, there are an odd number.

THE BUNGALOW

If we add up all the doors by which we could leave each room, then every inner door gets counted twice – making an even number. So the remainder, also even, must lead out.

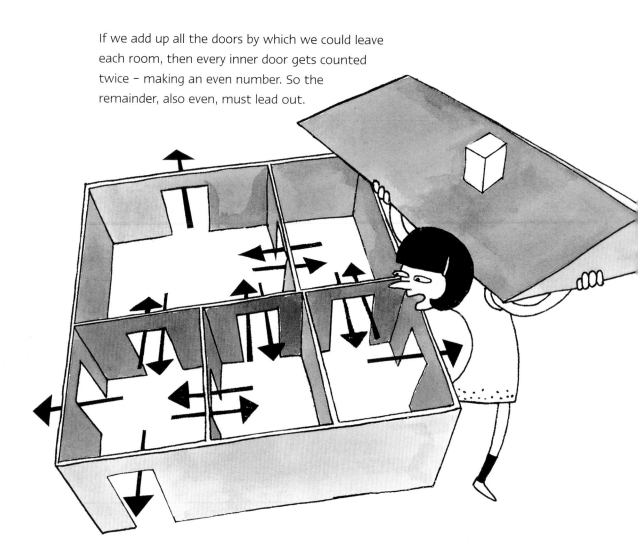

VARIATION

She calls the number of inner doors INNER and the number of outer doors OUTER. In the counting process, she counts inner doors twice and the outer ones only once. Her total is therefore two lots of INNER (which makes an even number) plus one lot of OUTER.

total doors = (2 × INNER) + OUTER

So to make an odd total, OUTER must be odd; and to make an even total, OUTER must be even.

THE CONFERENCE

A large number of people attend a conference. As each person meets someone he or she knows they shake hands. No one knows everyone, and some people may know no one, so we cannot say how many handshakes a particular person makes.

Prove that the number of people who shake hands an odd number of times is even.

You may find this quite difficult!

The solution does depend on just odd and even, but we have to go a stage further because the question talks of the number of people who shake hands an odd number of times. Try to get that clear in your mind first, and try it out with some small numbers. When you are sure you know – so sure you could explain it to someone else – then you may turn the page and check the answer.

CONFERENCE

THE CONFERENCE

GRAND TOTAL

82

Imagine that everyone has a counter on their head, which records handshakes.

GRAND TOTAL

84

Every shake adds 2 to the grand total, so that total must be even.

THE CONFERENCE

When everyone has finished greeting, put all those with an even number on their head to one side and those with an odd number to the other.

The counters with even numbers will clearly add up to make an even number, so we now need the counters with odd numbers to sum to an even number, to have an even grand total.

A collection of odd numbers can only add up to an even number if there are an even number of odd numbers. OK? Think about it.

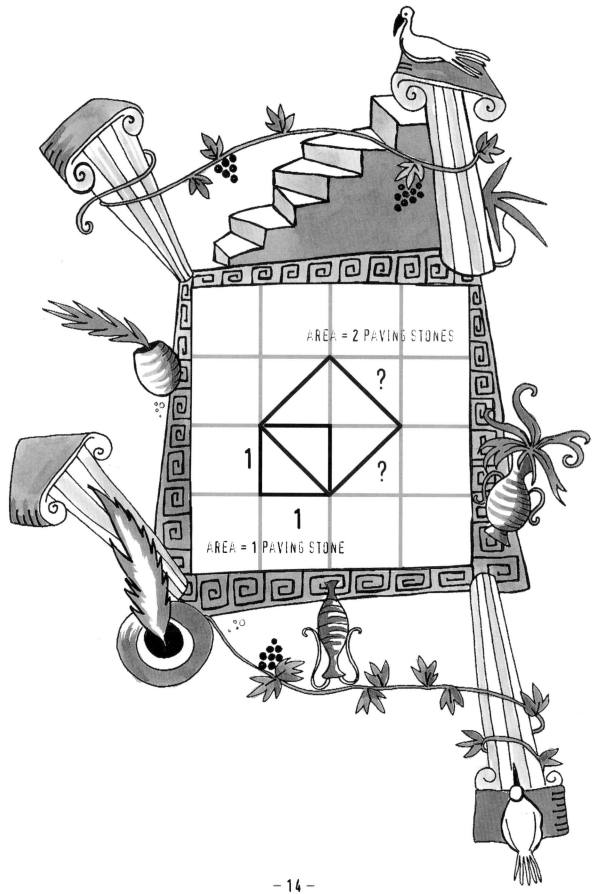

AREA = 2 PAVING STONES

?

1

?

1

AREA = 1 PAVING STONE

THE SQUARE ROOT OF TWO

The ancient Greeks liked only whole numbers and simple fractions. They were astonished when they found that you could not get a fraction that when multiplied by itself gave 2. The proof that there is no fraction is very short, but if you get it you are a genius... let me know!

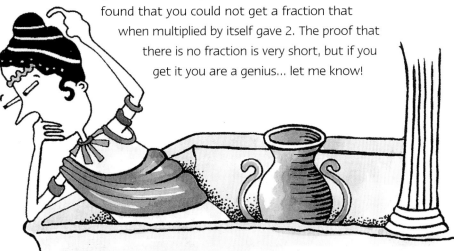

The Greeks found the absence of a nice number particularly frustrating as they did find a *line* which they could 'multiply by itself' (that is, draw a square on) to give an area of 2.

Imagine we are standing in a paved courtyard, like the one opposite; let's count the edge of a paving stone as 1, and its area as 1 square. Can we draw another square which has an area of 2 paving stones? How long is its edge?

We can try using an edge of 2, but this gives us an area of 4. And if we draw a square on an edge of $\frac{1}{2}$, we find $\frac{1}{4}$ of the paving stone.

In fact, we must draw the square on the diagonal of the paving stone. The area really is equal to 2 whole paving stones. But how long is the edge? You can keep trying, but you won't find a fraction that works!

The Greeks decided to describe the length of the diagonal as the SQUARE ROOT of 2: √2.

THE SQUARE ROOT OF TWO

Here's that actual proof that no fraction works. It is slightly different from the usual proof, as I have made it depend on odd and even.

Let's start by assuming the opposite (this is called PROOF BY CONTRADICTION). Suppose there *is* a fraction, written with two whole numbers, that we can square and get 2. Let's ask whether the top and bottom of the fraction are odd or even.

We need not look at $\frac{E}{E}$ because we can cancel this down until one of the numbers is no longer even.

So we only have to look at $\frac{O}{E}$, $\frac{O}{O}$ and $\frac{E}{O}$.

Take the first fraction and square it: $\frac{O^2}{E^2}$

Now see what happens if we claim that this makes 2.

$$\frac{O^2}{E^2} = 2$$

Multiplying both sides of the mathematical sentence by E^2 we have:

$$O^2 = 2 \times E^2$$

Now the left-hand side is odd and the right-hand side is even; so this fraction does not work.

Treating the next fraction similarly gives $O^2 = 2 \times O^2$

Again, the left-hand side is odd and the right-hand side even.

Finally, $E^2 = 2 \times O^2$

This time both sides are even, but the left-hand side is a multiple of 4 (can you see why?). So the left-hand side is 2 times an even number, and the right-hand side is 2 times an odd number: that fraction doesn't work either.

So there is no fraction that we can square to make 2.

THE BIG SQUARE

Draw a very large square, and divide it into identical small squares. Remove one small square from the top left-hand corner and another from the bottom right-hand corner.

Now take a large number of domino shapes, each covering two of the small squares.

Can you cover the shape with these dominoes, with no overlapping or spaces?

One of the solutions uses odd and even and is very long. Even if you get it, stop and think again, for there is another solution which is startlingly easy!

THE BIG SQUARE

If the big square is divided into an odd number of little squares, across and down, then the total number of little squares will be ODD. Even when we have removed the two corner squares, we are still left with an odd number, so we cannot possibly cover the grid exactly with dominoes.

What if the big square is divided into an even number of small squares across and down? Let's look at a 100 × 100 square, though the following arguments will actually work for any even number. We'll try the long-winded solution first.

SOLUTION 1

Let's assume we *can* cover the grid with dominoes – this is proof by contradiction again!

Remove the two corner squares as before: ROW 1 is left with an odd number of squares. However many dominoes we lay horizontally, these will cover an even number of squares. So there will be an odd number of gaps.

ROW 1

These have to be covered by vertical dominoes: an odd number of them.

The second row now has an odd number of squares left to cover, and the argument repeats.

THE BIG SQUARE

ROW 2

So ROW 2 has an odd number of dominoes hanging down.

We repeat this argument down to the row before last, in this case ROW 99. So ROW 99 also has an odd number of dominoes hanging down. ROW 100 cannot have any dominoes hanging down – it's at the bottom of the grid. We can cover the whole of ROW 100, however, as it has a corner missing and therefore an odd number of squares to fill.

Now let us count up the vertical dominoes. We have an ODD number (99 rows) of ODD numbers (hanging dominoes) to add up. The total is ODD, and that is the number of vertical dominoes.

Leaving the dominoes in place, turn the square through a right angle and repeat the argument. The dominoes that were horizontal are now vertical and, just as before, there will be an odd number of these. The total number of dominoes on the big square is therefore ODD plus ODD, which is EVEN.

But this cannot be true, since the big square (100 × 100, or any EVEN × EVEN) would have been covered by an even number of dominoes before we removed the corners; and therefore should now be covered with an odd number of dominoes.

So it is not possible to cover the big shape exactly with dominoes!

THE BIG SQUARE

I did the first solution and was gobsmacked when I heard this one.

SOLUTION 2

Colour the squares as in a chessboard. If the number of squares across and down is even, then the two removed are the same colour, say black.

Each domino should cover a black and a white square, but since there are now two fewer black squares than white, it cannot be done.

This is what is called lateral thinking.

PLAYING WITH NUMBERS

The branch of mathematics called NUMBER THEORY deals just with whole numbers but can be very difficult. Just for fun, let us look at two problems that no one has ever solved.

Goldbach's Conjecture says that every even number (there we are again!) greater than 2 can be written as the sum of two prime numbers.

Prime numbers, you remember, are numbers that can only be divided exactly by two different numbers: themselves and 1. Here are some examples of primes: 2, 3, 5, 7, 11, 13, 17, 19, 23.

Numbers which are not prime are called COMPOSITE.

Christian Goldbach posed his conjecture in 1742, in a letter to the brilliant mathematician, Leonhard Euler. Here is an even number where it clearly works:

$$88 = 5 + 83$$

And there may be other pairs of primes that add up to 88.

However, no one has ever been able to prove whether it is true for *all* even numbers or not. Of course, if someone found an even number where it couldn't be done, that would resolve the matter, but showing that it always works is more of a problem.

Another conjecture that has not been solved is this.
Take the square numbers: 1, 4, 9, 16, 25... It is believed, but has never been proved, that between successive square numbers you can always find a prime.

The problems that follow are not as difficult as that!

A quick reminder of two words, 'multiple' and 'factor':
15 is a multiple of 5; 5 is a factor of 15. Nice and symmetric.

$2^{6972593} - 1 = 437075744$

WHERE ARE THE PRIMES?

At the time of writing, the largest known prime is $2^{6972593} - 1$
It has 2 098 960 digits, and was found on 1 June 1999 by an
American called Nayan Hajratwala. Hajratwala was one of thousands
of people across the world using spare computer time to run the
Great Internet Mersenne Prime Search – and after 111 days his
machine popped up a prime.

GIMPS has found four huge primes so far and will probably find
more, so if you have a computer and would like to get involved,
take a look at www.mersenne.org/prime.htm. All of the software
is free, and you will be part of an international network doing real
mathematical research.

There are also lots of questions in the mathematical world about the
distribution of the primes, but I have one very simple problem for you.

Prove that every prime from 5 onwards sits next to a multiple of 6
(that is, that the prime is one above or one below a multiple of 6).

WHERE ARE THE PRIMES?

We should equip our minds with pictures of numbers. One important picture is the PEBBLE image, where we see numbers as separate counters or pebbles. Cricket umpires count the bowling with pebbles in their pockets.

The other important image is the NUMBER LINE, where numbers sit in order on a line, which we can move along. This is the picture we will use for this problem.

Take a stretch of number line anywhere you fancy, like this.

The stars mark the multiples of 6.

Since 6 is even, the points marked with an oval are even...

...and the points halfway between the 6s, marked with blocks, are multiples of 3.

The only place we could possibly find numbers that are not composite is next to the multiples of 6, so that is where the primes must be.

SQUARE NUMBERS

The problem: why can you not have a remainder of 2, when a square number is divided by 3?

SQUARE NUMBERS

Let's start by sorting all numbers according to what happens when we divide them by 3. We find that every whole number is either an exact multiple of 3, leaves a remainder of 1 over, or has a remainder of 2. Get that?

Now get the squares by squaring each of these types of number.

Multiples of 3 remain multiples of 3.

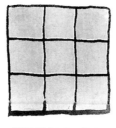

MULTIPLE OF 3

MULTIPLE OF 3

A number which has a remainder of 1 becomes another multiple of 3, plus 1.

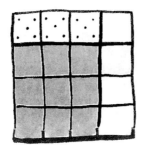

MULTIPLE OF 3, PLUS 1

MULTIPLE OF 3, PLUS 1

And a number with remainder 2 gives a multiple of 3, plus 4. When you divide this leftover 4 by 3, you get remainder 1.

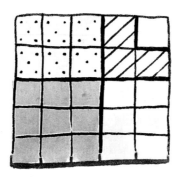

MULTIPLE OF 3, PLUS 1

MULTIPLE OF 3, PLUS 2

So a remainder of 2 is not possible.

BASKET CASE

A girl goes into a supermarket and buys four items. Using a calculator she multiplies the prices (in pounds), instead of adding them. At the checkout she says, "So that's £7.11," and the checkout man, correctly adding the items, agrees.

What were the prices of the four items?

BASKET CASE

Let's treat £7.11 as 711p to find the factors. Trial and error gives us
711 = 3 × 3 × 79.

So 7.11 = 3.00 × 3.00 × 79.00 × 0.01, but this doesn't sum to 711p.

Let's try writing it as common fractions:

$$7.11 = 3 \times 3 \times 79 \times \frac{1}{100} \text{, or}$$

$$7.11 = 3 \times 3 \times 79 \times \frac{1}{(2 \times 2 \times 5 \times 5)}$$

And now we can mess around with all sorts of arrangements, as
long as any fraction we introduce cancels to $\frac{1}{1}$.

$$7.11 = 3 \times \frac{3}{2} \times \frac{79}{(2 \times 5)} \times \frac{1}{5} \text{, or}$$

$$7.11 = 3 \times \frac{3}{2} \times 79 \times \frac{1}{(2 \times 5 \times 5)} \times \frac{3}{3} \times \frac{5}{5},$$

and so on.

As in most number theory problems, a certain amount of trial and
error is involved. One thing to consider is that prices can only have
two decimal places, so we have to stick to fractions such as $\frac{3}{4}$ or $\frac{6}{5}$.

THE MARTIAN

Just a quickie to remind us that all may not be as it seems.

We show a Martian eight objects and ask her to write down the number. She writes **12**.

How many fingers does she have on each hand?

THE MARTIAN

Obviously the Martian number base is 6. So most people say Martians have three fingers on each hand.

This is totally wrong. They have two fingers on each of three hands.

Some problems are designed to mislead the reader.

LOGIC

Problems that involve straight reasoning can be tackled with no knowledge of mathematics at all. In fact, it is problems where you have had no teaching that show how good you are.

Sophie Germain decided to become a mathematician at the age of 13. Her parents were so angry that a nice Parisian girl of 1789 should be reading maths books, that they took away her light and even her clothes. In India, a century or so later, Srinivasa Ramanujan did have maths lessons at school, but then couldn't go to university because of illness and lack of money. He was also 13 when, in 1900, he started working mathematics out for himself.

The dramatic stories of how both became famous mathematicians include a kilogram of gold, a surprise letter to Cambridge University and Napoleon's invasion of Germany. Find out more at www-history.mcs.st-and.ac.uk/~history/

This chapter includes ideas from some mathematical thinkers who specialised in logic.

CROCODILES

Here is a problem by Lewis Carroll, the author of *Alice's Adventures in Wonderland*. He was around in the 19th century but this type of logic problem is much older. It was devised in Greece by Aristotle, around 350 BCE, and is called a SYLLOGISM.

Deduce the deepest possible conclusion from these three statements.

A Babies are illogical.

B Nobody is despised who can manage a crocodile.

C Illogical persons are despised.

CROCODILES

This can be figured out purely with words.

C and **A** together mean that babies are despised.
B means that people who are despised cannot manage a crocodile.
So babies cannot manage a crocodile.

THE WASON PROBLEM

This is more recent. It was developed in the 1960s by Peter Wason, a psychologist at University College in London, to test peoples' powers of reasoning.

You know that these four cards each have a letter on one side and a number on the other.

You are also given this statement about the four cards.

> If a card has an odd number on one side,
> then it has a vowel on the other side.

You are asked to find out if this statement is true. How many cards, and which, must you turn over to be sure?

THE WASON PROBLEM

We try to prove that the statement is not true. Clearly we should start by turning the **3**.

If there is no vowel on the back of the **3**, then the statement is immediately refuted.

If there *is* a vowel, we still don't know that the statement is true for *all* the cards.

If we turn the **C** and find an odd number, this is also a refutation.

If it is an even number, do we know the statement is true yet?

Well, **A** is a vowel. But the statement only requires that '**ODD** leads to **VOWEL**'. We have no information about '**VOWEL** leads to...'. So turning over the **A** tells us nothing. Similarly, we don't know any restrictions on even numbers, so turning the **4** also doesn't matter for the statement.

So we will know whether the statement is true or not after turning at most two cards – the **C** and the **3**.

DUCKS

You know that every healthy duck is greedy and every old duck is greedy. You also know that, on a particular farm, some ducks are greedy and some are not.

Which of the following statements about the ducks on that farm *must* be true?

1 There are both young ducks and old ducks.

2 All the ducks that are not greedy are young.

3 Some of the young ducks are sick.

4 All the sick ducks are young.

DUCKS

Some of you will reason it out just with words, but it may be helpful to use set diagrams. These ones are called **VENN DIAGRAMS**, after the mathematician John Venn. (Born in Hull in 1832, Venn was also a dab hand at engineering: his automatic bowling machine for cricket was a real cracker.)

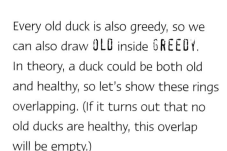

We know every healthy duck is greedy, so the **HEALTHY** set lies inside the ring marked **GREEDY**.

Every old duck is also greedy, so we can also draw **OLD** inside **GREEDY**. In theory, a duck could be both old and healthy, so let's show these rings overlapping. (If it turns out that no old ducks are healthy, this overlap will be empty.)

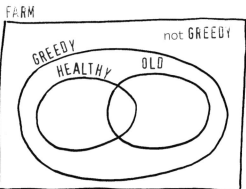

And on the whole farm, some ducks are greedy and some are not. So there are definitely ducks somewhere inside the **GREEDY** set, and other ducks outside.

So which of the four statements must be true, and which could be false?

1 We have drawn the **OLD** ring, but do not know whether there are actually ducks in it. Statement 1 could be **FALSE**.

2 All ducks that are not greedy lie outside the **GREEDY** ring, and are therefore outside **OLD**. Statement 2 must be **TRUE**.

3 We know there are definitely ducks outside **GREEDY**, so these must be both sick and young (as they cannot be **HEALTHY** or **OLD**). Statement 3 must be **TRUE**.

4 There is a region for sick and **OLD**, which could well have a duck in (although we are not sure!). Statement 4 could be **FALSE**.

ORANGES AND LEMONS

A greengrocer receives three boxes labelled ORANGES, LEMONS and ORANGES & LEMONS. He is told that there was a mix up at the fruit depot, and all the labels are on the wrong boxes.

How can he tell where each label ought to be by picking just one piece of fruit out of a single box (but without looking inside any of the boxes)?

ORANGES AND LEMONS

He picks one piece of fruit from the box labelled ORANGES & LEMONS.

If it is a lemon, then that box should actually say LEMONS. The box labelled ORANGES can't contain just oranges, and must really be the mixed one. This leaves the box labelled LEMONS to contain oranges.

How should the greengrocer label the boxes if the piece of fruit is an orange?

FRIENDS AND STRANGERS

If there are six people in a room, show that there must be at least three who all know each other, or at least three who are mutual strangers.

Assume that if person **A** knows person **B**, then **B** also knows **A**. (Of course, this would not be true if **A** were a secret agent spying on **B**!)

FRIENDS AND STRANGERS

Let's label the six people **0, A, B, C, D, E.**

Join **0** to the other people. Label these five lines with **F** (to show the person is a friend of **0**) or **S** (to show they are strangers).

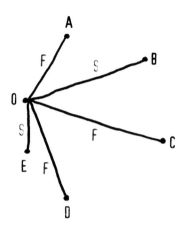

At least three lines will be of the same sort (think about it!). First time round, let's suppose it is **F**.

Take the three friends of **0** – in these diagrams **A, C** and **D** – and join them up. Now label each line in the triangle you have just made **F** or **S**.

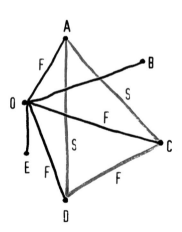

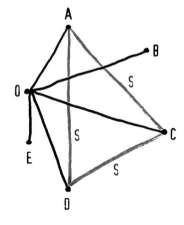

If any side of triangle **ACD** shows a friend, then we have made a friends triangle, here **0CD**. So these three people all know each other.

If no side of triangle **ACD** shows a friend, then clearly **A, C** and **D** are three mutual strangers.

Go back and follow the whole argument again, swapping **S** for **F**: you will still get three friends or three strangers.

The result is proved!

HOUSE NUMBERS

Avtar lives in a house with a number between 10 and 1300.
Billie knows this, and asks him questions.

Chelsea also knows this, and is standing next to Billie with her
personal stereo on. She can hear Billie's questions, but not Avtar's
answers. However, she knows from his face when he is lying.

Billie: "Is it above 500?"   QUESTION 1
Avtar answers (and lies).

Billie: "Is it a perfect square?"   QUESTION 2
Avtar answers (and lies).

Billie: "Is it a perfect cube?"   QUESTION 3
Avtar answers (truthfully).

Billie thinks for a while. "OK, this will decide it," she says.
"Is the second digit 1?"   QUESTION 4
Avtar answers (but Chelsea doesn't see whether he is lying or not).

Billie: "Then your number is... "   QUESTION 5
(But Chelsea doesn't hear Billie's number.)
Avtar: "No, it isn't."

Chelsea: "Now I know what your number is."

What is Avtar's house number?

HOUSE NUMBERS

I hope you started by listing of all the square and cube numbers; you will need them for what follows...

Now then. If Avtar had claimed that his house number was neither a square nor a cube, Billie would not have thought she was near an answer after three questions.

If he had answered that the number was both a square and a cube, Billie would have believed it to be **64** or **729**, and would not have asked **QUESTION 4**

If Avtar had said that the number was a square but not a cube, Billie would have had more than two possible choices, so again she wouldn't have decided to ask **QUESTION 4**.

Therefore Avtar must have told Billie that his number was not a square but is a cube.

Billie now asks what she thinks is a deciding question.

Looking at the cubes, the only way to get a choice of just two numbers is if Avtar had answered 'yes' to **QUESTION 1**, and Billie is now trying to decide between **512** and **1000**.

If Avtar says 'yes' to the last question, Billie will announce that his number is **512**, and if 'no' that it is **1000**. And either way she will be wrong!

So Chelsea knows that Avtar's answers were: 'above 500', 'not a square' and 'yes, a cube'. And she knows that in truth, the number is below 500, is a square and is a cube.

CHELSEA KNOWS...

☆ Avtar said the number was a square or a cube, but not both.

☆ Avtar did not say 'the number is a square but not a cube'.

☆ In truth, the number is a square and is a cube.

☆ Billie must be down to two numbers.

☆ The true answer to **QUESTION 1** should have been 'no, not above 500'.

☆ Avtar's house number is **64**.

HOUSE NUMBERS

You might also find it helpful to draw a tree diagram.

1) ABOVE 500? 2) SQUARE? 3) CUBE? 4) 2ND DIGIT IS 1?

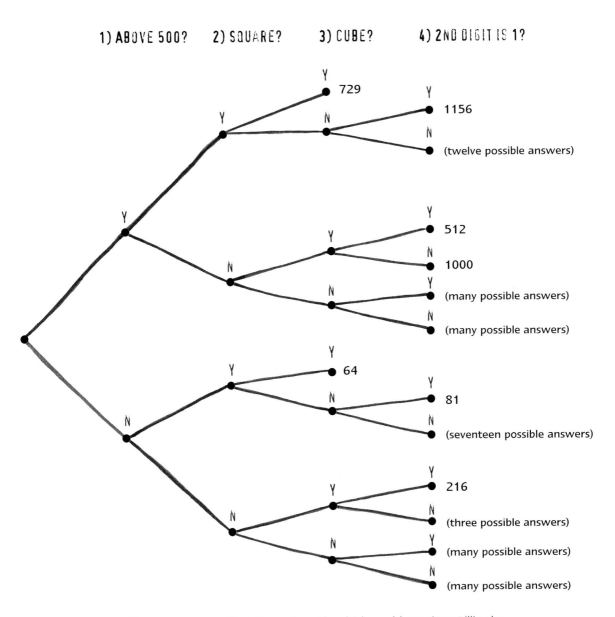

Now we can see that the only path which could convince Billie she would get Avtar's number with QUESTION 4 was YES, NO, YES, and then YES or NO. So the true path was NO, YES, YES – and we have an answer in three questions.

MAKING TABLES

We saw in the previous chapter that it is sometimes helpful to make lists and draw diagrams. A lot depends on how your mind works; mathematical understanding is a very personal thing. I once taught two best friends, one of whom only understood numbers and equations, and the other of whom could only think in diagrams and mental images.

But remember – systematic approaches are not a substitute for actual *thinking*!

SCORES

In a computer game, you score 7 points for every phial of potion you find and 11 points for every jewel you collect. There is no limit to the number of jewels and phials of potion you can collect.

What scores can you *not* make?

VARIATION

The cost of posting a parcel depends on its weight. What values can you not make using only 9p and 15p stamps?

You will find a hint for these at plus.maths.org/issue15/puzzle. In fact, you may like to check out the whole of the *Plus* magazine, and NRICH Online Maths Club, both at nrich.maths.org/index.html.

SCORES

We have to start by looking at the scores we *can* make, and then we will know which ones we can't – complements again.

Let's arrange the numbers in rows of 11. We know we can get any score in the right-most column as it's a multiple of 11, so we'll shade that column. We can also definitely make any multiple of 7, so let's shade those numbers in red.

Once we can make a particular number, we can also make any score below it in the table – by collecting additional jewels. So we can make all the shaded numbers. The highest impossible score is 59.

1	2	3	4	5	6	7	8	9	10	11
12	13	14	15	16	17	18	19	20	21	22
23	24	25	26	27	28	29	30	31	32	33
34	35	36	37	38	39	40	41	42	43	44
45	46	47	48	49	50	51	52	52	54	55
56	57	58	59	60	61	62	63	64	65	66
67	68	69	70	71	72	73	74	75	76	77
78	79	80	81	82	83	84	85	86	87	88

VARIATION

Both 9p and 15p are multiples of 3p, so we can't make *any* number that isn't a multiple of 3 (why not?). To see which other values we can't make, let's arrange the numbers in rows again, this time up to 15.

(We need only include the multiples of 3, since the other numbers are impossible anyway.)

3	6	9	12	15
18	21	24	27	30
33	36	39	42	45
48	51	54	57	60

The only extra impossible values are 3, 6, 12 and 21.

LINES AND SQUARES

This 2 × 6 grid has a total of 10 straight lines and 17 squares. Can you find them all?

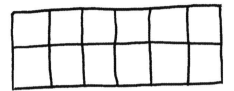

This 3 × 4 grid has 9 straight lines and 20 squares. Again, can you find them all?

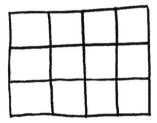

Find the smallest number of lines needed to make exactly 100 squares.

LINES AND SQUARES

You might get this one by luck. If not, try looking at patterns in the number of lines and squares in grids of different sizes.

Let's look at 2 × n grids (where n means 'any number').

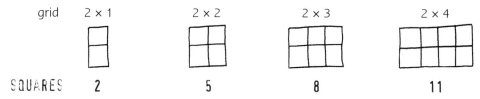

grid	2 × 1	2 × 2	2 × 3	2 × 4
SQUARES	2	5	8	11

The SQUARES numbers form a pattern of 'add 3'.

How about a 3 × n grid?

grid	3 × 1	3 × 2	3 × 3	3 × 4	3 × 5
SQUARES	3	8	14	20	26

The pattern of the SQUARES numbers settles to 'add 6'.

For a 4 × n grid the sequence again becomes regular from around the square grid: 4, 11, 20, 30, 40, 50, 60, 70, 80, 90, 100. Aha! SQUARES reaches 100 at a 4 × 11 grid (which has 5 + 12 lines). But 17 may not be the smallest number of lines with which we can make 100 squares. Keep checking!

The 5 × n pattern goes: 5, 14, 26, 40, 55, 70, 85, 100.
The 5 × 8 grid has 6 + 9 lines, and 15 does indeed turn out to be the lowest number of lines, even if you keep looking.

If you want to know where these patterns of 'add 3', 'add 6' and so on come from, look at the number of unit squares, four-squares, nine-squares... that are added each time you increase n by 1.

ANYONE FOR TENNIS?

A knock-out tennis tournament has entries from 137 players. The organiser is not sure how to arrange this number of players, so he pairs off as many entrants as he can and gives one bye (that is, one person goes through to the next round without having to play). He repeats this every round.

How many matches have to be played?

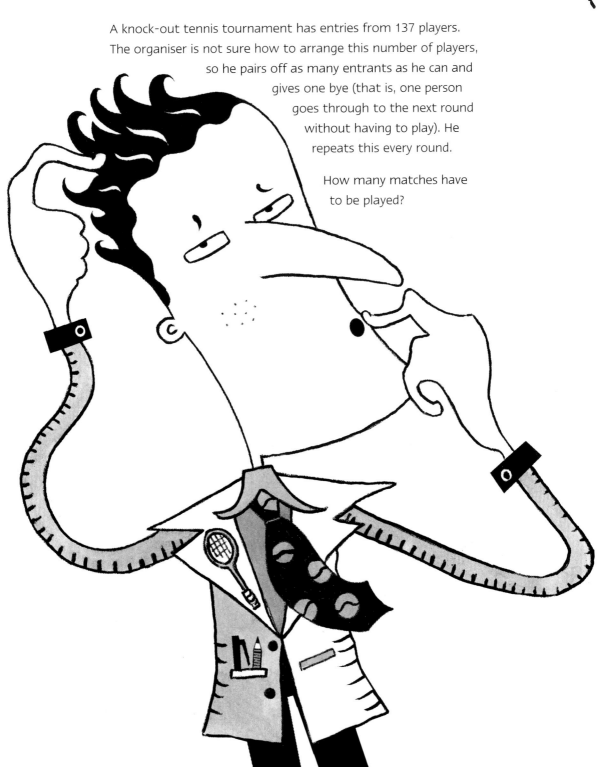

ANYONE FOR TENNIS?

This is another example of a problem designed to mislead you.

The problem encourages you to follow the organiser's path. In the first round he pairs off 136 of the players into 68 matches, plus one person over. He then has 69 people. He pairs off 68, giving 34 + 1, and so on.

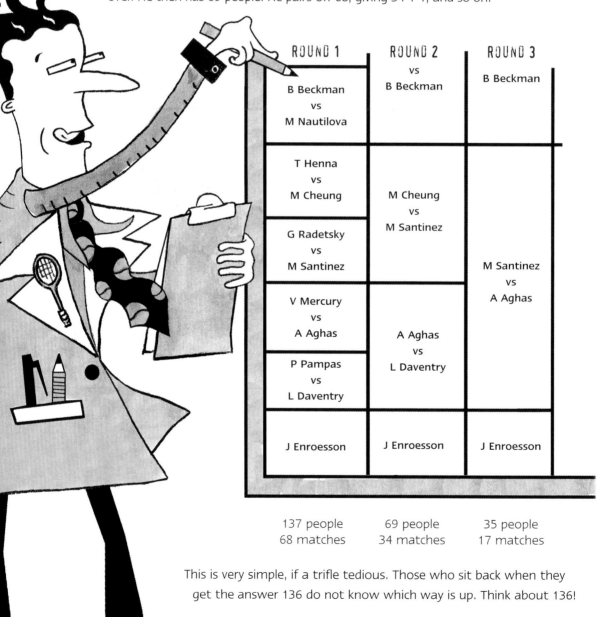

ROUND 1	ROUND 2	ROUND 3
B Beckman vs M Nautilova	vs B Beckman	B Beckman
T Henna vs M Cheung	M Cheung vs M Santinez	
G Radetsky vs M Santinez		M Santinez vs A Aghas
V Mercury vs A Aghas	A Aghas vs L Daventry	
P Pampas vs L Daventry		
J Enroesson	J Enroesson	J Enroesson
137 people 68 matches	69 people 34 matches	35 people 17 matches

This is very simple, if a trifle tedious. Those who sit back when they get the answer 136 do not know which way is up. Think about 136!

ANYONE FOR TENNIS?

However many people there are and however you arrange matches, each match knocks out one player. That is why it is 136 – but you should have got that answer immediately.

As a matter of interest, big tournaments like Wimbledon only admit an exact power of 2 (such as 128) so that there need be no byes unless people drop out at the last moment. If you had 137 entrants, you should subtract that from the next highest power of 2, which is 256, giving 119. If you give that number of byes in the first round and only play off the remaining 18 players that will give you 9 + 119 (= 128) players. So from the second round onwards no bye is needed.

If you did need further byes (perhaps because of injury), you should certainly not give them all to the same person! Our organiser will let J Enroesson go straight through to the final without playing a match!

THE DUD COIN

You have twelve coins. You know one is a dud and is a different weight from the others. You have a balance but no weights. What is the least number of weighings you need to find the dud and determine whether it is light or heavy?

This is one of several famous 'dud coin' problems – some rather cunning. During a war, one side once suggested feeding a coin problem to the other side, to puzzle their spies and keep them busy.

THE DUD COIN

Split the coins into three piles
of four and label them.

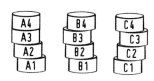

Weigh pile **A** against pile **B**. 1ST WEIGHING
There are three possible cases: piles **A** and **B** weigh the same;
pile **A** weighs more than pile **B**; or pile **B** weighs more than pile **A**.

CASE 1

If pile **A** weighs the same as pile **B**,
then all of these coins are the same
and the dud is in pile **C**. Relabel each
A and **B** coin with **S** for standard.

Now weigh **C1** and an **S** against
C2 and **C3**. 2ND WEIGHING

CASE 1:1

If **C1** plus **S** equals **C2** plus **C3**, then **C4** is the dud. Whether it is light
or heavy can be tested against an **S**. 3RD WEIGHING

CASE 1:2

If **C1** plus **S** weighs more than **C2** plus **C3**, then either **C1** is heavy or
one of **C2**, **C3** is light. That is, one of them is the dud.

Weigh **C2** against **C3**. 3RD WEIGHING
If they are the same, the dud must be **C1** and is heavy. If they are
different, whichever is lighter is the dud.

CASE 1:3

If **C1** plus **S** weighs less than **C2** plus **C3**, follow the same argument
as CASE 1:2 but swap 'heavy' and 'light'.

Now to the next possibility.

THE DUD COIN

CASE 2

If pile **A** weighs more than pile **B**, then either an **A** coin is heavy or a **B** coin light. So the **C**s are all standard: label these **S** instead.

Weigh **A1**, **B1** and **S** against **A2**, **A3** and **B2**. **2ND WEIGHING**

CASE 2:1

If **A1**, **B1** and **S** equal **A2**, **A3** and **B2**, then the dud must be **A4** (heavy) or one of **B3** and **B4** (light).

Weigh **B3** against **B4**. **3RD WEIGHING**

If these weigh the same, then the **A4** is indeed a heavy dud; if different then the lighter coin is the dud.

CASE 2:2

If **A1**, **B1** and **S** weigh more than **A2**, **A3** and **B2**, then either **A1** is heavy or **B2** is light. Weigh one against **S**. **3RD WEIGHING**

CASE 2:3

If **A1**, **B1** and **S** weigh less than **A2**, **A3** and **B2**, then either **B1** is light or one of **A2** and **A3** is heavy. Weigh **A2** against **A3**. **3RD WEIGHING**

CASE 3

If pile **B** weighs more than pile **A**, the argument is like **CASE 2** with the **A**s and **B**s swapped. We can say that **CASE 3** proceeds from **CASE 2** by **SYMMETRY** (and **CASE 1:3** from **1:2**).

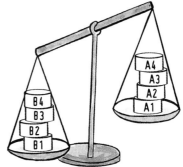

In all cases the dud – and whether it is heavy or light – can be found in exactly three weighings.

THE DUD COIN

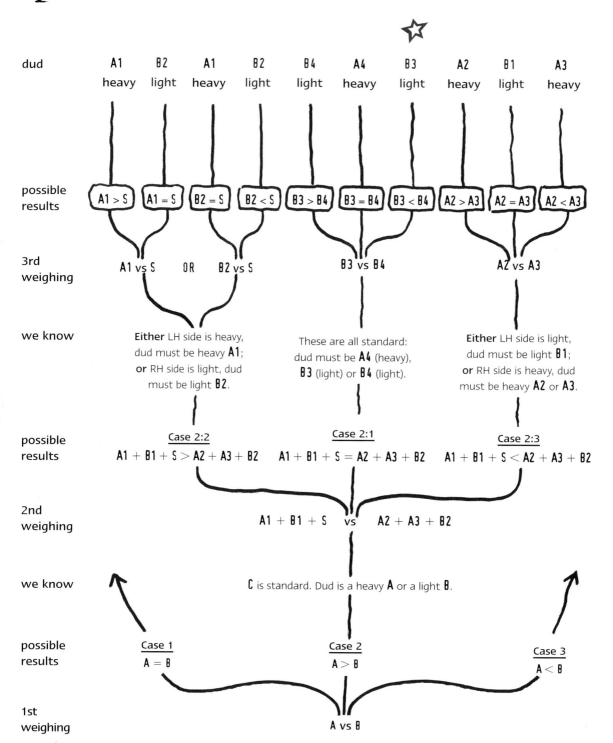

dud	A1 heavy	B2 light	A1 heavy	B2 light	B4 light	A4 heavy	B3 light	A2 heavy	B1 light	A3 heavy

possible results

A1 > S | A1 = S | B2 = S | B2 < S | B3 > B4 | B3 = B4 | B3 < B4 | A2 > A3 | A2 = A3 | A2 < A3

3rd weighing

A1 vs S   OR   B2 vs S   B3 vs B4   A2 vs A3

we know

Either LH side is heavy, dud must be heavy **A1**; **or** RH side is light, dud must be light **B2**.

These are all standard: dud must be **A4** (heavy), **B3** (light) or **B4** (light).

Either LH side is light, dud must be light **B1**; **or** RH side is heavy, dud must be heavy **A2** or **A3**.

possible results

Case 2:2
A1 + B1 + S > A2 + A3 + B2

Case 2:1
A1 + B1 + S = A2 + A3 + B2

Case 2:3
A1 + B1 + S < A2 + A3 + B2

2nd weighing

A1 + B1 + S   vs   A2 + A3 + B2

we know

C is standard. Dud is a heavy **A** or a light **B**.

possible results

Case 1
A = B

Case 2
A > B

Case 3
A < B

1st weighing

A vs B

VISUALISING SHAPES

You may find these questions easy, or completely impossible. If shapes and images come naturally to you, this is for you. On the other hand, if you are the same sort of thinker as Ramanujan (for whom the whole numbers were all personal friends) you may have some difficulty.

You have been warned!

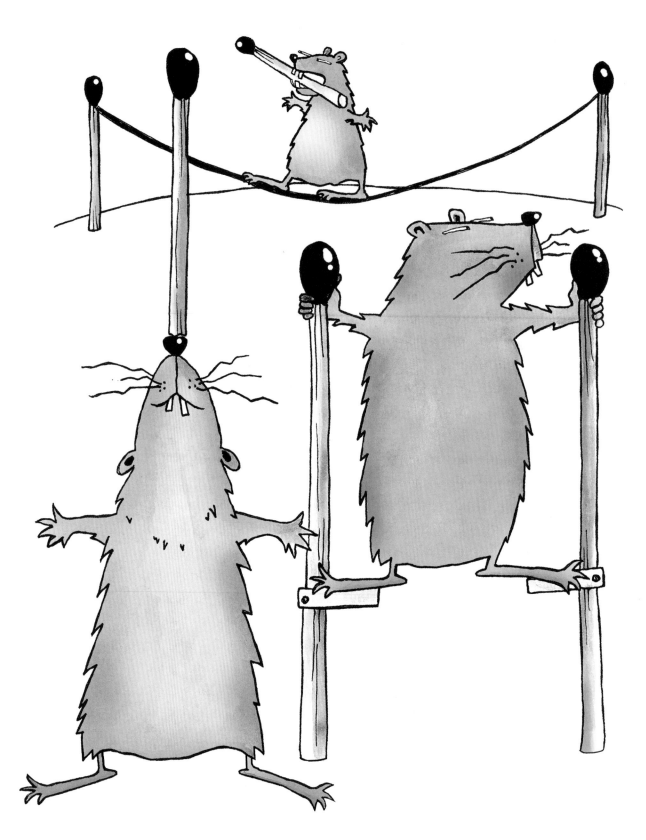

MATCHSTICKS

You have six matchsticks. Arrange them so they form four equilateral triangles.

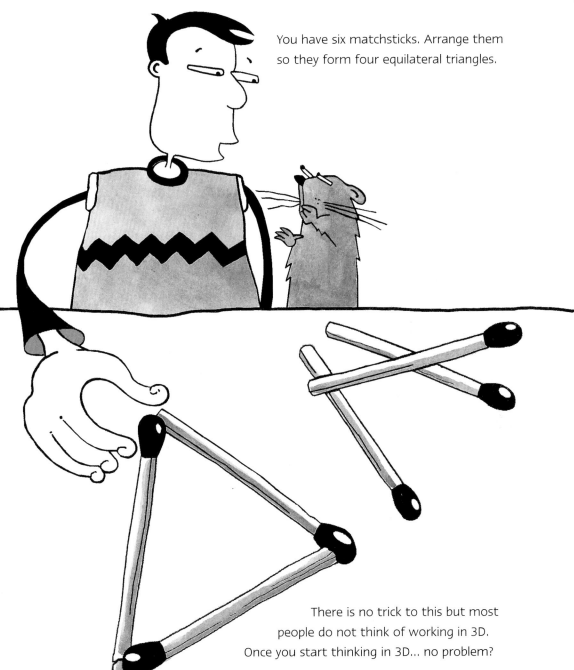

There is no trick to this but most people do not think of working in 3D. Once you start thinking in 3D... no problem?

MATCHSTICKS

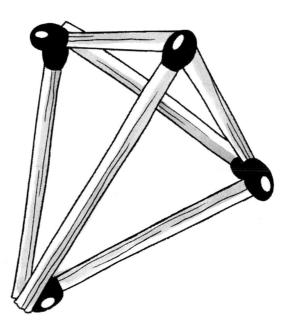

Bingo!

Another puzzle designed to mislead!

ALL IN THE MIND

Suspend a cube from one vertex and allow it to hang freely. Lower it into water until it is exactly half submerged. What shape does the surface of the water make round the cube?

You must do this in your mind without other help.

ALTERNATIVE

Find all the ways that a single slice across a cube leaves a square showing.

ALL IN THE MIND

You are only allowed to do this mentally. When you have failed, do it practically and you will see that it is a regular hexagon.

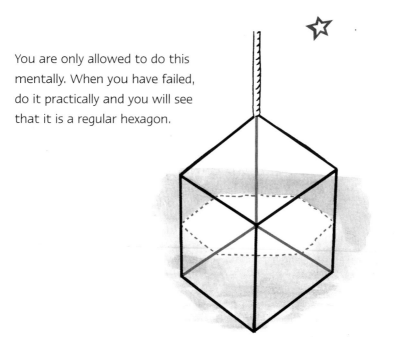

This is a very telling method of determining a person's power of visualisation. One child of 7 gave the answer immediately and, when asked how he did it, said dismissively, "I just put it up in my mind, turned it around and and looked at it."

I have known three people (two with a degree in mathematics) who have no ability of visualising and cannot even see a cube in their minds.

ALTERNATIVE

Parallel to a face... or imagine a stick of equal length to a side, laid across the top of the cube so that its ends are on edges. Cut straight down.

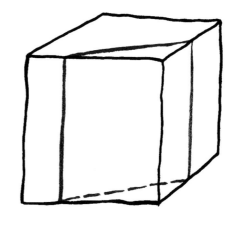

THE NORTH POLE PROBLEM

Where on earth can you travel a mile south, a mile west
and a mile north and be back where you started?

THE NORTH POLE PROBLEM

I called this the North Pole problem as a joke. I was first told it when I was 10, and it was stated that an explorer set out, went a mile south, a mile west and a mile north and was back at his tent, where he found a bear. What colour was it? When the answer came back that he must be at the North Pole and the bear therefore white, I fell about laughing.

Many years later a friend gave me the problem without the bear. I answered offhandedly, "The North Pole."

"Yes," she said, "and where else?"

So if you got the North Pole, think again.

THE NORTH POLE PROBLEM

After a quarter of an hour I said, "Anywhere on a circle a mile north of a circle around the South Pole of circumference a mile." I was very chuffed.

" Yes," said she, "and where else?" Plonk!

THE NORTH POLE PROBLEM

Draw a set of circles of circumferences 1 mile, $\frac{1}{2}$ mile, $\frac{1}{3}$ mile, $\frac{1}{4}$ mile... around the South Pole, and another set a mile north of each of these. The explorer could have started on any of the latter.

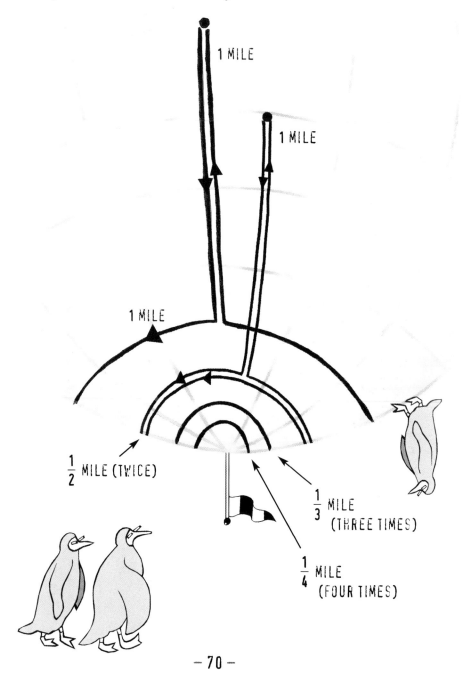

1 MILE

1 MILE

1 MILE

$\frac{1}{2}$ MILE (TWICE)

$\frac{1}{3}$ MILE (THREE TIMES)

$\frac{1}{4}$ MILE (FOUR TIMES)

CUBIST CUTS

A 3 x 3 x 3 cube may be reduced to unit cubes by six saw cuts, if you go straight at it. If after every cut you can rearrange the pieces before cutting straight through, can you do it in fewer?

Answer the same question with a 4 x 4 x 4 cube, and then an n x n x n cube.

CUBIST CUTS

This is beautiful!

The central cube of the 27 has six faces, each of which must be cut separately. So it cannot be done in fewer than six cuts.

The 4 × 4 × 4 cube is a big surprise. It still only take six cuts! Think why.

Do one vertical cut through the centre. Place one piece on top of the other and a second cut can split the cube into four 'walls'.

CUBIST CUTS

Do this in each of three ways and you have reduced the 4 × 4 × 4 to unit cubes. Two cuts in each of three directions is six cuts.

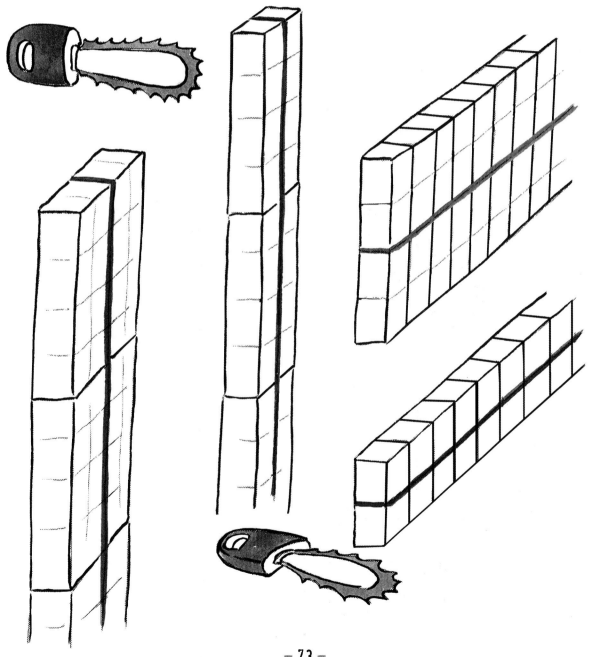

CUBIST CUTS

And the n × n × n cube?

For 5 ≤ n ≤ 8 (that is, n is a number between 5 and 8, inclusive) it takes nine cuts: three in each direction.

For 9 ≤ n ≤ 16 it takes twelve cuts.

For each doubling of n, you can cut the cube up completely for only three extra cuts (as long as your saw is long enough!).

A COUPLE MORE

Mathematical thinking takes many forms. The problems so far have been grouped according to the underlying ideas. The next two are a bit weird. The thinking is (perhaps) mathematical, but I am not sure what mathematics is.

TRAIN TIMES

When I get up in the mornings, which is at random times, depending on what I was doing the previous night, I set off for the station. I do not bother what time it is, but just catch the first train that comes. I live out in the sticks and there is just one train an hour each way. The trains are regular, but don't arrive at the station together. One direction takes me to work, the other takes me to the sports centre.

I have explained my principle to my boss, and asked that she pay me for half of each week, on the grounds that I might end up at either place each day. She agreed to this at first, but after the first six weeks we found I had done a total of just one week's work. She thinks I'm cheating, but I have promised her I'm not. I genuinely do not notice the time in the morning, and I do take the first train, and the timetable hasn't changed.

She still does not think I ought to go to the sports centre five days out of six, and I can't blame her. How does it happen?

TRAIN TIMES

We did not mention how long I have to wait for a train. The trains heading for the sports centre come on the hour, every hour. Those that go to work come at 10 minutes past the hour, every hour.

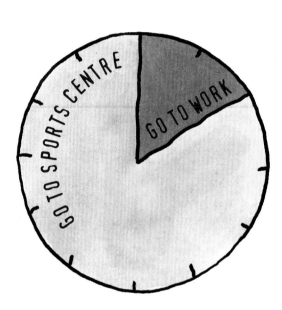

So if I arrive at random times, I am five times as likely to go to the sports centre as to work.

I hope they do not rearrange the timetables!

NEW YORK

Are there two people in New York with the same birthday? Why?

NEW YORK

Yes, although we don't know which day(s) it is.

There are (at most) 366 days in the year, and there are more than 366 people in New York – so they cannot all have different birthdays.

Interestingly, if I specify the date ("Are there two people in New York with a birthday on 23 March," say) then the answer might be 'no'. We can't be sure that there is even one person in New York with a birthday on that day – unless I cheat and give you my friend's birthday, of course!